PROS AND CONS

THE DEBATE ABOUT PAYING
COLLEGE ATHLETES

by Gail Terp

FOCUS
READERS

www.focusreaders.com

Focus Readers is distributed by North Star Editions:
sales@northstareditions.com | 888-417-0195

Produced for Focus Readers by Red Line Editorial.

Photographs ©: Tony Quinn/Icon Sportswire/AP Images, cover, 1; Sean Locke Photography/Shutterstock Images, 4–5; Monkey Business Images/Shutterstock Images, 7, 44; Photo Works/Shutterstock Images, 8–9; Red Line Editorial, 10, 34; August_0802/Shutterstock Images, 12; lithian/Shutterstock Images, 14–15; Junial Enterprises/Shutterstock Images, 16; lutherhill/iStockphoto, 19; Aspen Photo/Shutterstock Images, 20–21, 26–27; Rocketclips, Inc./Shutterstock Images, 23; Martial Red/Shutterstock Images, 24; Blend Images/Shutterstock Images, 29; aabejon/iStockphoto, 31, 45; BarakBlueSky/Shutterstock Images, 32–33; NASA, 37; James Marvin Phelps/Shutterstock Images, 38–39; Mike Broglio/Shutterstock Images, 41; aceshot1/Shutterstock Images, 43

ISBN
978-1-63517-523-3 (hardcover)
978-1-63517-595-0 (paperback)
978-1-63517-739-8 (ebook pdf)
978-1-63517-667-4 (hosted ebook)

Library of Congress Control Number: 2017948097

Printed in the United States of America
Mankato, MN
November, 2017

ABOUT THE AUTHOR

Gail Terp is a retired elementary teacher who writes for kids and beginning adult readers. Her books for kids cover history, science, animals, and biography. When not reading and writing, she walks around looking for interesting stuff to write about. She lives in Upstate New York.

TABLE OF CONTENTS

CHAPTER 1

AN INTRODUCTION TO COLLEGE ATHLETICS

In many colleges, sports play an important role in the life of the school. Some top division college teams become famous. Students, parents, and other community members buy tickets to games and cheer for their teams. TV stations broadcast the games for fans at home. Sporting goods companies supply the players' equipment. This is a good way to advertise their brands. The top teams bring in huge amounts of money.

For many colleges, sports games serve as large social events.

Each year, college sports earn hundreds of millions of dollars for their schools.

Student athletes are the reason colleges take in all this money. If athletes didn't play, there would be no ticket sales. TV stations would have no college games to broadcast. Currently, many college athletes receive free **tuition**. But they do not share in the money that their colleges earn from the games. This has led to a heated debate. Should college athletes be paid for playing? Some people believe it's only fair that student athletes receive a share of the money they helped generate. Others think paying college athletes would interfere with the athletes' schooling.

Many groups are involved in this debate, including athletes, coaches, and colleges. The owners of TV stations and sporting goods companies have opinions, too. Another group

▲ In 2015, 47 percent of people in the United States followed college sports.

involved in the debate is the National Collegiate Athletic Association (NCAA). The NCAA is the organization in charge of college sports in the United States. It writes and enforces the rules for each sport.

The issue of paying college athletes is complex. The stakes are high for all who are involved. Both sides have strong arguments for their views.

CHAPTER 2

PRO
ATHLETES DESERVE A PORTION OF THE MONEY THEY GENERATE

The money that athletes generate for their colleges comes from several sources. Ticket sales for games bring in money. Fans also buy **merchandise**, such as team shirts and other products with team names and logos on them. In addition, **alumni** donate money to the sports programs of the colleges they once attended.

TV stations pay colleges large sums of money to broadcast games. One example is basketball.

The top Division I basketball teams in the NCAA compete in the March Madness tournament.

In 2016, a TV network agreed to pay the NCAA $8.8 billion dollars for the right to broadcast the men's basketball tournament from 2024 to 2032.

NCAA rules determine how an athlete's name, photo, or likeness can be used. The schools may use them in advertisements and on merchandise. They may hang posters with athletes' names and

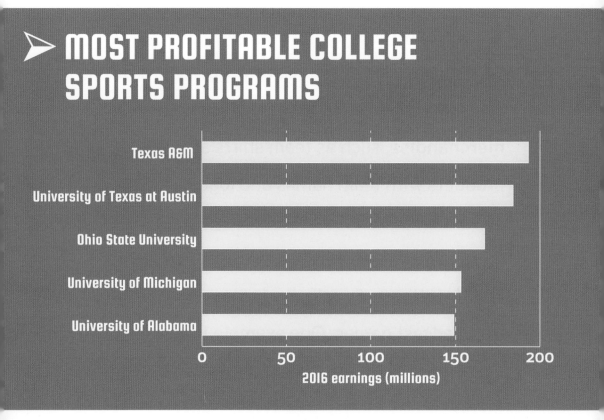

MOST PROFITABLE COLLEGE SPORTS PROGRAMS

2016 earnings (millions)

pictures to advertise upcoming games. They may also sell jerseys for their teams' top players. Some schools even sell video games with the likenesses of their top players. Any profits from the sale of these products go to the schools or to the NCAA. NCAA rules ban student athletes from profiting from any of these sales.

Advocates for paying college athletes believe athletes should share in the wealth they generate for their schools. After all, it is the athletes' performance on the field that creates profit opportunities. Therefore, the athletes should earn more than only their **scholarships**.

DID YOU KNOW? ◄

Coaches earn a portion of the money that their programs take in. In 2016, the top five coaches in college sports earned between $6 million and $9 million.

⬩ Shoe companies often use athletes to advertise their products.

However, not everyone agrees on the best method for paying athletes. Some suggest that colleges pay each athlete a minimum salary, such as $25,000 per year. Another idea is to let athletes earn money for each game they play.

Some people believe athletes should receive a share of the money their names, photos, and likenesses earn. For instance, if a video game uses a basketball player's likeness, the athlete should share in the game's profits. If football players sign autographs at a sporting goods store, they should be allowed to accept pay from the store's owner.

Not all advocates agree on how athletes should be paid. But they do agree that receiving payment is fair. Discussions will continue regarding the best way to make fair payments.

ATHLETIC SCHOLARSHIPS VS. PROFESSIONAL SALARIES ◁

College athletes often dream of playing for professional teams. Going pro means athletes can continue doing what they love. It also means they'll earn lots of money. An average yearly sports scholarship is approximately $22,000. Players of major pro sports earn an average of $2 million yearly. Top players earn far more than that.

CHAPTER 3

PRO
LONG-TERM SCHOLARSHIPS SUPPORT ATHLETES' EDUCATIONS

College athletes spend long hours involved in their sports. NCAA rules state that practice sessions should take no more than 20 hours each week. However, practice sessions are not athletes' only sports-related activities. Athletes often have lengthy trips traveling to and from games. They also watch video of practice sessions, looking for ways to improve. They take part in workouts. They attend team meetings. They compete in games.

College athletes often lack the time and energy for studying.

△ Many athletes must do strength training in addition to their regular practice hours.

These time commitments can add up to more than 40 hours per week.

Advocates for pay think student athletes should be paid for their hard work. However, salaries are not the only options for payment. Many advocates think colleges should pay athletes through educational support. This support would come in the form of long-term tuition payments.

Sports often leave student athletes with little time for academics. In the time they have left for classwork, athletes are often too tired to do their best. Student athletes who don't maintain strong grades may lose their scholarships.

Many schools offer tutoring to student athletes. However, this support isn't always enough. Some schools take other steps to improve athletes' grades. They encourage athletes to take easy classes. They may arrange for others to do athletes' assignments. Unlike tutoring, these actions do not help athletes learn. When caught, schools receive fines and other punishments.

Many colleges attempt to support athletes' educations through one-year scholarships.

DID YOU KNOW? ◁

Athletes often believe they can't complain about having no time to study. They worry their coaches will cancel their scholarships if they do.

However, these scholarships pose problems. One-year scholarships must be renewed each year. Coaches can choose not to renew them if an athlete is not performing as well as they'd like. If athletes' coaches decide to cancel their scholarships, the athletes must pay their own tuition. Many athletes cannot afford the cost of tuition. This makes attending college impossible.

In contrast, multiyear scholarships can last for two to five years. These scholarships continue even if the athlete is no longer able to play. However, multiyear scholarships are uncommon. Most colleges only offer one-year scholarships to student athletes.

Many advocates for pay think athletes should be paid through long-term scholarships. They propose eliminating one-year scholarships. They want all athletic scholarships guaranteed for at

College athletes earn scholarships by playing well in high school.

least four years. That way, athletes do not have to worry about paying for their schooling.

Some advocates think scholarships alone are not enough. They want a system that helps student athletes manage their workloads. This system would allow athletes to take fewer classes each term. Their scholarships would then be extended for up to eight years. This would enable hard-working athletes to earn their degrees.

CHAPTER 4

PRO
PAYMENT OF MEDICAL COSTS HELPS ATHLETES RECOVER FROM INJURY

Practice sessions can be long and punishing for college athletes. Preseason practices start weeks before the first games of the season. And for some sports, practice begins in the heat of summer. Players work on skills and weight train for strength. They play practice games. When the official season begins, players practice less. Although fewer in number, these sessions are still intense.

Injuries can happen during practice sessions, warm-ups, or games.

Practice is important for preparing athletes for competition. However, practice sessions can also lead to injuries. Advocates for paying college athletes believe colleges, or the NCAA, should pay for athletes' medical costs. These payments would help injured athletes receive the treatment they need.

Some athletic injuries are minor and involve a short recovery time. Others are more serious and require long recovery times. For example, some athletes injure their anterior cruciate ligament (ACL). This injury affects the knee and often requires surgery. Recovery from an ACL injury takes many months before an athlete is able to play again.

A concussion is a type of brain injury caused by a hard blow to the head. It is among the most serious injuries athletes face. Concussions cause

▲ Doctors look at a patient's eye movement when testing for a concussion.

many **symptoms**, including headaches, nausea, and depression. When an athlete has had several concussions, the symptoms can be long lasting.

To play on a college team, athletes must carry medical **insurance** that covers athletic injuries. Unfortunately, this insurance doesn't always cover all expenses. As a result, the families of injured athletes may have high medical bills.

Long-term injuries can create a heavy financial burden on families. Recovery from concussions

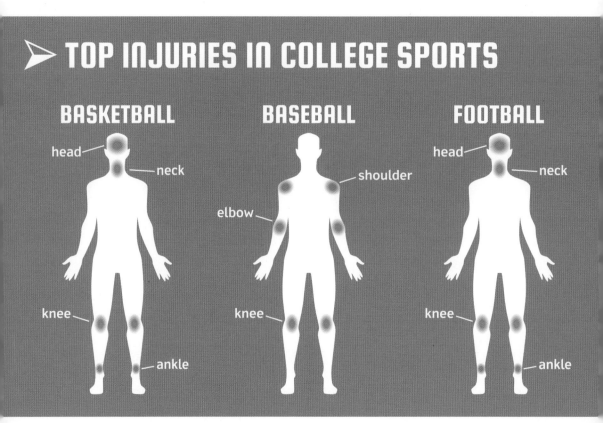

➤ TOP INJURIES IN COLLEGE SPORTS

BASKETBALL
head—
—neck
knee—
—ankle

BASEBALL
—shoulder
elbow—
knee—

FOOTBALL
head—
—neck
knee—
—ankle

and other injuries can take years. In some cases, injuries may affect players for the rest of their lives. Some colleges provide financial help for long-term injuries. However, most do not.

Many former student athletes have brought **lawsuits** against their colleges and the NCAA. These athletes suffer from the long-term effects of concussions. They claim their schools didn't protect them from the dangers of concussions. The courts have to decide whether these athletes should receive money for their medical costs.

Advocates for pay want colleges, or the NCAA, to pay for athletes' medical insurance. This insurance would cover all sports injuries. If an athlete gets injured during any sports activity, insurance would pay for the athlete's full treatment. It would also cover the long-term effects from injuries for as long as they continue.

CHAPTER 5

CON

ATHLETES ARE ALREADY PAID THROUGH SCHOLARSHIPS AND BENEFITS

Opponents of paying college athletes believe short-term scholarships are payment enough. College programs in at least 35 sports offer scholarships to student athletes. Scholarship sports include archery, baseball, golf, soccer, tennis, and many more. The highest one-year men's scholarship in 2016 was in basketball. The player received $53,075. The highest women's scholarship was in gymnastics for $63,337.

In 2015, the average track and field scholarship for women in Division I of the NCAA was $15,905.

However, most scholarships are not that high. The average is between $10,000 and $30,000.

Most of the scholarship money a student receives pays for tuition, plus **room and board**. Scholarships also usually pay for students' books. These can be expensive. Recently, NCAA rules permitted colleges to offer athletes a **stipend**. Athletes can use stipends to pay for school

➤ POSTSEASON AWARDS

NCAA rules forbid schools to give athletes money awards during the sport season. However, the rules do allow cash awards at the end of each season. In all sports, schools can give athletes up to $425 per year for sports participation. If a team plays in a championship contest, each player can also receive up to $375. Athletes in a bowl or all-star game can receive cash or gifts valued up to $550.

The average cost of room and board at four-year public colleges in the 2016–2017 school year was $10,440.

expenses that their scholarships don't cover. Stipends are typically $3,000 to $7,000 per year.

Most college students have high debts when they graduate. The average debt for a college graduate in 2017 was approximately $27,000. It can take students years to pay this money back. Therefore, athletic scholarships give athletes a financial advantage over many other students.

Some college athletes who have scholarships graduate with no student debt.

College athletes receive many benefits in addition to scholarships. For instance, they get to work with top coaches and learn skills in their sports. They also train in state-of-the-art facilities. Football teams often have huge indoor practice fields. And sports buildings contain first-class weight rooms. There are **hydrotherapy** rooms to treat sore muscles and injuries. There are also rooms for athletes to relax in, many of which have high-end video systems. These sports facilities are only for student athletes. Some schools and coaches think these benefits work as substitutes for athlete pay.

An opportunity to attend college offers more than academic benefits. College campus life is rich with many opportunities. Students can go to

▲ At some schools, special equipment allows athletes to train underwater.

museums and engage in other art experiences. They can attend concerts, dances, and theater performances. Many athletes also become involved in the community. Some volunteer in schools near their college. Others raise funds for people in need. These campus opportunities offer college athletes valuable experiences and worthwhile skills.

CHAPTER 6

CON
PAYMENTS PUT THE FOCUS ON ATHLETICS OVER ACADEMICS

The NCAA values the importance of graduation for all student athletes. To compete, athletes must meet certain academic standards each year. They must take a required number of courses each semester and maintain passing grades. Student athletes who do not meet these requirements are not eligible for competition.

Some people worry that paying college athletes would draw athletes' focus away from academics.

Many college athletes strive to succeed in sports and earn their degree.

College athletes are supposed to focus on being a student first and an athlete second. Very few student athletes go on to play professional sports. But student athletes who graduate gain many benefits in the job market.

 **GOING PRO**

Percentage of NCAA student athletes who go on to play for a major professional team (2017)

Sport	NCAA Participants	Percentage Who Go Professional
Men's Baseball	34,554	9.1%
Men's Basketball	18,684	1.1%
Women's Basketball	16,593	0.9%
Men's Football	73,660	1.5%
Men's Hockey	4,102	5.6%
Men's Soccer	24,803	1.4%

Professional athletes are paid to win games. Paying college athletes would place pressure on athletes to perform like professionals. Student athletes might think that winning is the top priority. They may start taking sports more seriously than school. Without a firm focus on academics, most students will never graduate.

Student athletes have job advantages when they graduate from college. College graduates tend to earn more and have better health benefits. They are also less likely to be unemployed. In addition, many employers like to hire former college athletes. Companies want employees who are team players. They look for individuals who can work toward goals and persevere through failure. Employers also want workers who know how to manage their time. Athletes typically have all these skills.

Many former athletes credit sports for their success after school. For example, Tom Catena played football in college before becoming a doctor. As a student athlete, Catena learned time-management and teamwork skills. Another example is astronaut Nicole Mann, who played soccer in college. College sports taught Mann how

➤ COLLEGE ATHLETE GRADUATE RATES

The NCAA keeps track of graduation rates for college athletes. According to the NCAA's Graduation Success Rate (GSR) scale, graduation rates have increased since 2002. The 2002 graduation rate for student athletes was 74 percent. The 2016 rate had increased to 86 percent. The GSR is used only for student athletes. It cannot be compared with the nonathlete student graduation rate.

Nicole Mann (front row, right) was a member of the 2013 class of NASA astronauts.

to balance multiple responsibilities. They also taught her to focus.

College sports are not about money. Students should be able to focus on more than winning. As college athletes, they have the unique opportunity to build skills for the future. Playing for money, or simply to win, takes away the true spirit of sports. It also fails to prepare students for their future.

CHAPTER 7

CON

PAYMENT METHODS ARE UNFAIR TO SOME COLLEGES AND STUDENTS

Some colleges earn lots of money from their sports programs. They use the money to pay for training facilities, coaches, and general college expenses. These schools could probably afford to pay their athletes. However, athlete salaries would take funds away from other important uses.

Most colleges do not earn money from their sports. These colleges maintain sports programs with money from their general college budgets.

Men's lacrosse is one of five NCAA championships that make as much money as they cost to run.

If schools were forced to pay their athletes, other items in their budgets would suffer. Some schools may have to raise tuition rates and give fewer scholarships. If paying athletes became too difficult, some schools might do away with sports altogether.

If the NCAA allows colleges to pay student athletes, colleges must decide which athletes should receive a salary. They could decide to pay every athlete. However, some sports do not earn money for schools. Athletes of sports that do make a profit, such as football and basketball, may think this is unfair. After all, it's their sport

> DID YOU KNOW?

The majority of Division I college sports programs lose money for their schools.

⚠ Many college water polo programs struggle from a lack of funding.

that earns the school money. Colleges could decide to pay only football and basketball players. But athletes of other sports might think this is unfair. After all, they also work hard and put in long hours. Finding a payment method that is fair to all athletes would be difficult.

Nonathlete students may also think paying student athletes is unfair. Many colleges charge students an athletics fee. Colleges use this fee to support their athletic programs. Athletic fees can be several hundred dollars per year. Many students have complained about paying this fee. They may be more upset if their money is used to pay student athletes.

If colleges decide to pay athletes, other issues of fairness would arise. Schools would have to determine how much to pay athletes. They could pay all athletes the same amount. Or they could base athletes' pay on the number of games they play. Salaries could even be based on athletes' grades.

Each payment method creates its own problem. For example, one option is to base athletes' pay on the amount of money they earn for the school.

▲ The Ohio State Buckeyes attract top players from around the country.

But then, colleges with top teams could offer athletes as much as they wanted. Top athletes would choose the school that would pay them the most. This would give schools with more resources an unfair advantage. Schools with fewer resources would no longer be able to compete.

PROS

- College athletes deserve a portion of the money generated through ticket sales.
- Schools should pay athletes when using their faces or names on promotional materials.
- College athletes should be paid for their hard work and long practice sessions.
- Schools should provide more long-term scholarships so athletes have time to graduate.
- Student athletes are at risk of injury every time they play. Colleges should cover all medical costs for treatment of injuries.

CONS

- Student athletes already receive scholarships that cover tuition, room, and board.
- College sports programs offer benefits instead of pay, such as training with top coaches.
- Paying college athletes would draw athletes' focus away from school.
- Paying college athletes would put too much focus on winning and making money.
- If colleges pay athletes, schools might have to raise tuition or cut school programs.
- No payment method would be fair to all colleges and students.

PAYING COLLEGE ATHLETES

Write your answers on a separate piece of paper.

1. Write a one-paragraph summary of the ways college sports generate money.

2. Do you think college athletes should be paid? Why or why not?

3. What is the average range of a stipend for college athletes?

    A. $10,000 to $30,000
    B. $6 million to $9 million
    C. $3,000 to $7,000

4. How does the NCAA affect the debate about paying college athletes?

    A. Colleges must follow the NCAA's rules.
    B. The NCAA must follow colleges' rules.
    C. The NCAA's main priority is making money for schools.

Answer key on page 48.

GLOSSARY

alumni
Previous students of a particular school, college, or university.

hydrotherapy
The use of water to treat injury or disease.

insurance
Money paid by a company or organization to cover certain types of costs, such as medical treatment.

lawsuits
Conflicts between two people or groups that are taken to court.

merchandise
Manufactured goods that are bought and sold.

room and board
A place to live and food to eat.

scholarships
Money given to students to pay for educational expenses.

stipend
A periodic payment.

symptoms
Signs of an illness or disease.

tuition
A sum of money students pay to attend college.

TO LEARN MORE

BOOKS

Basen, Ryan. *Injuries in Sports*. Minneapolis: Abdo Publishing, 2014.

Forest, Christopher. *The Kids' Guide to Sports Ethics*. North Mankato, MN: Capstone Press, 2014.

Tatarsky, Daniel. *Infographic Guide to Sports*. London: Cassell Illustrated, 2014.

NOTE TO EDUCATORS

Visit **www.focusreaders.com** to find lesson plans, activities, links, and other resources related to this title.

INDEX

Answer Key: 1. Answers will vary; **2.** Answers will vary; **3.** C; **4.** A